hjbnf   HEB
611.2 GODDU

Goddu, Krystyna Poray author
Major Organs
33410015141411   03/05/19

D1713015

Hebron Public Library
201 W. Sigler Street
Hebron, IN 46341

The Amazing Human Body

MAJOR ORGANS

KRYSTYNA PORAY GODDU

WORLD BOOK

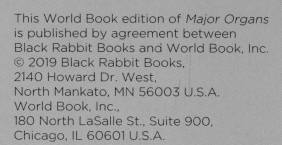

This World Book edition of *Major Organs* is published by agreement between Black Rabbit Books and World Book, Inc.
© 2019 Black Rabbit Books,
2140 Howard Dr. West,
North Mankato, MN 56003 U.S.A.
World Book, Inc.,
180 North LaSalle St., Suite 900,
Chicago, IL 60601 U.S.A.

All rights reserved. No part of this book may be reproduced in any form without written permission from the publisher.

Jennifer Besel, editor; Grant Gould, designer; Omay Ayres, photo researcher

Library of Congress Control Number: 2017020390

ISBN 978-0-7166-3434-8

Printed in China. 3/18

Image Credits

Alamy: Oliver Burston, 6–7;
Getty: Dorling Kindersley, 15:
iStock: comotion_design, 31; lukaves, 18-19; Olena_Kravchenko, Cover, 29 (heart);
Science Source: 3D4Medical, 21; Shutterstock: Africa Studio, 13; Alila Medical Media, 8; Anton Nalivayko, 24-25; Billion Photos, 4–5; CLIPAREA l Custom media, 29 (t); decade3d - anatomy online, 16; Lightspring, 12, 32; Magic mine, 28 (b); Nerthuz, 22; patrice6000, 11 (bkgd); Ralf Juergen Kraft, Cover, 29 (skeleton); Sebastian Kaulitzki, 1, 3, 11 (brain), 28 (t); Stephen Mcsweeny, 26; Vector for u, Cover (bkgd)

Every effort has been made to contact copyright holders for material reproduced in this book. Any omissions will be rectified in subsequent printings if notice is given to the publisher.

CONTENTS

CHAPTER 1

Introduction to
ORGANS

The heart pounds. The lungs take in air. The stomach **digests** food. The body's organs do their jobs all day. And their work keeps a person alive.

The human body has many different organs. But what are organs? They are groups of millions of **cells**. And those cells all do specific jobs. • • • • • • • • • •

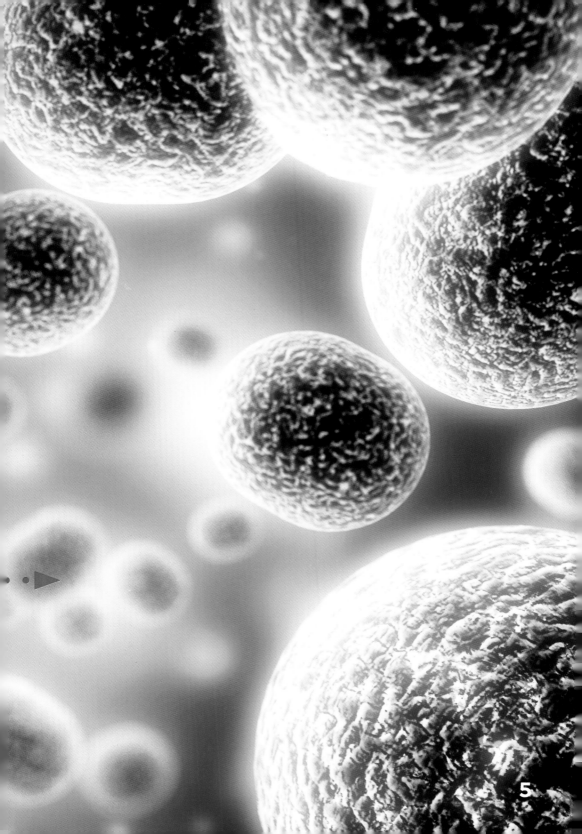

SOME MAJOR ORGANS

eye

heart

brain

skin

lung

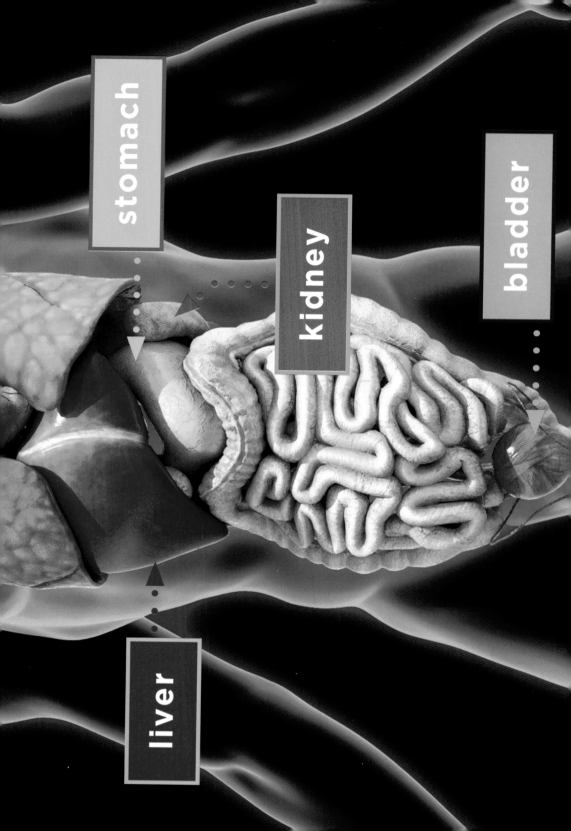

stomach

bladder

kidney

liver

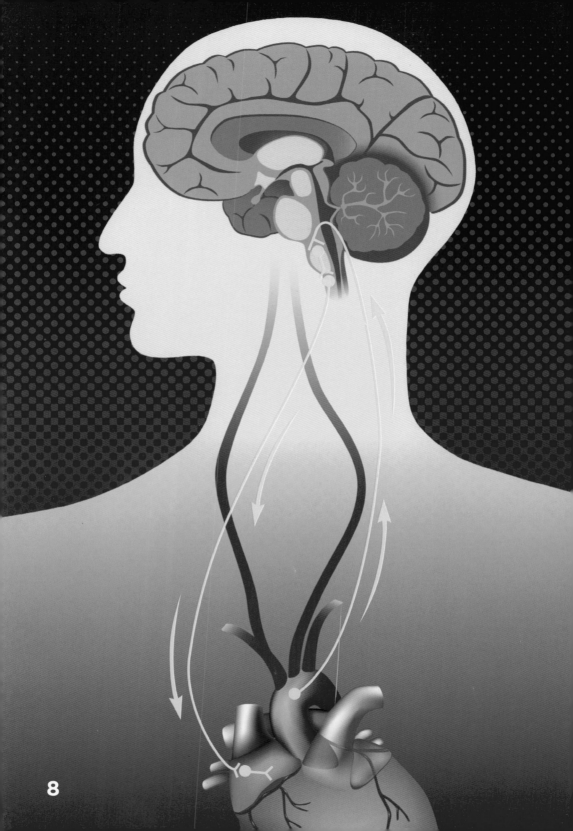

8

CHAPTER 2

The BRAIN and the Heart

The brain and the heart are two well-known organs. Without these two, other organs couldn't do their jobs.

The brain is the control center of the body. It sends **electrical** signals to body parts. Those signals tell the lungs to breathe. They tell the heart to beat. People don't have to tell these organs to work. The brain does that automatically.

Parts of the Brain

The brain is divided into parts. One part is for thoughts and memories. Another part controls movement. The brain stem sends the signals that keep other organs going.

cerebellum
(balance and movement)

· · · · ▶

cerebrum
(thoughts and memories)

brain stem

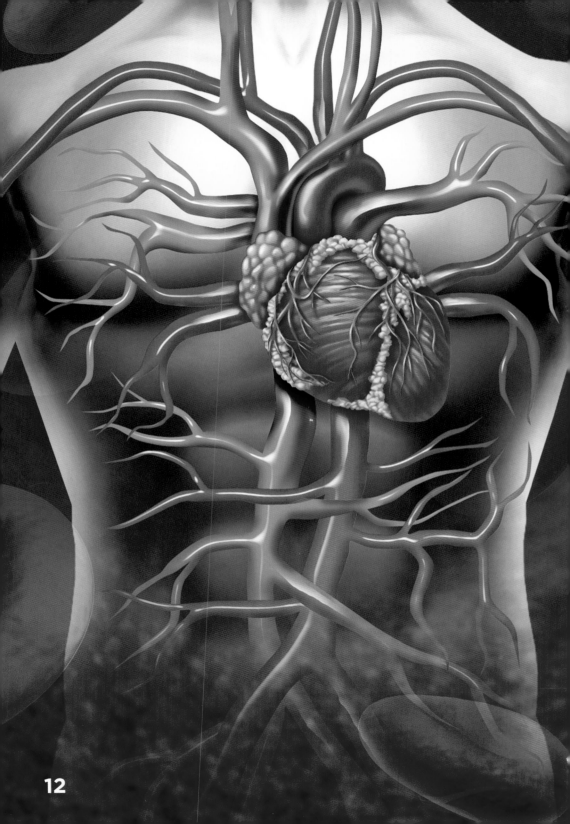

The Heart's Job

The heart is a big muscle in the chest. It pumps blood through the body. If the heart stops pumping, the body can't stay alive.

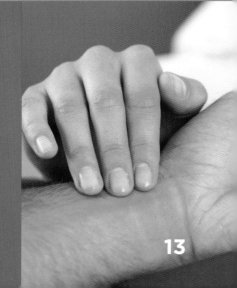

Doctors check patients' pulses. They are checking to see how fast the heart is pumping. A fast or slow pulse might signal a problem.

13

The Blood Cycle

An adult has about 1 gallon (4 liters) of blood. The heart keeps all the blood moving. Blood travels into the right side of the heart. The heart pumps the blood to the lungs. The lungs fill blood with **oxygen**. Then they send it to the heart's left side. The left side pumps the oxygen-filled blood throughout the body.

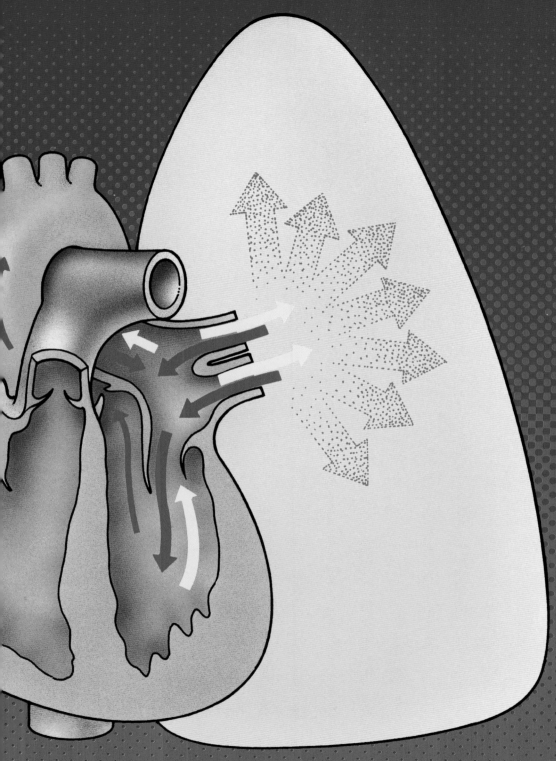

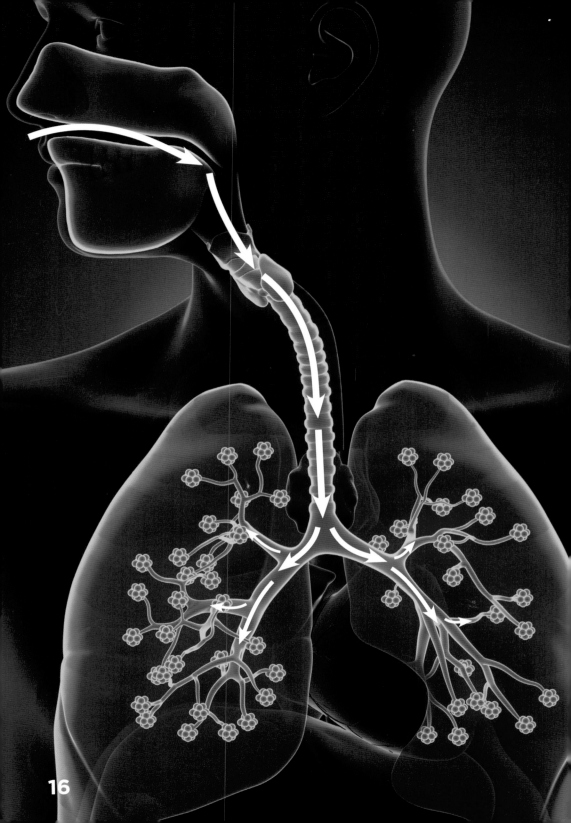

In and

Some organs bring in things the body needs. Other organs take things out. The lungs and kidneys are two such organs.

Air enters the body through the nose or mouth. It travels into the two lungs. There, they give blood oxygen. Old air makes a reverse trip out of the body.

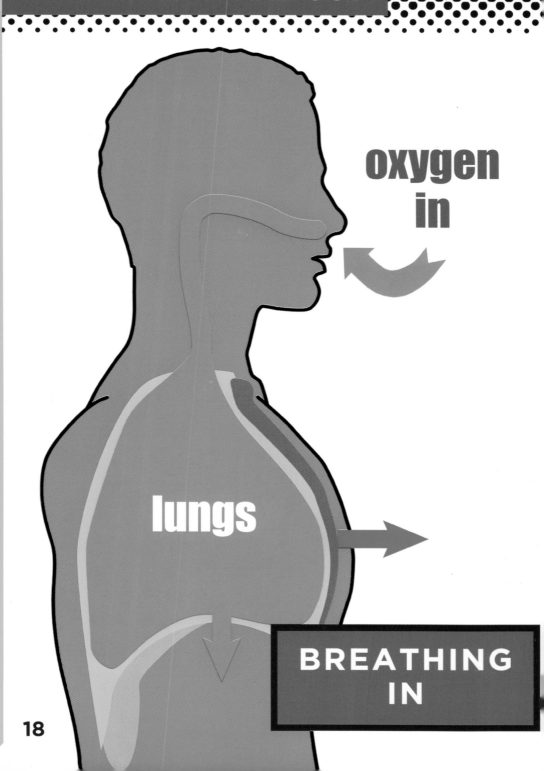

oxygen in

lungs

BREATHING IN

18

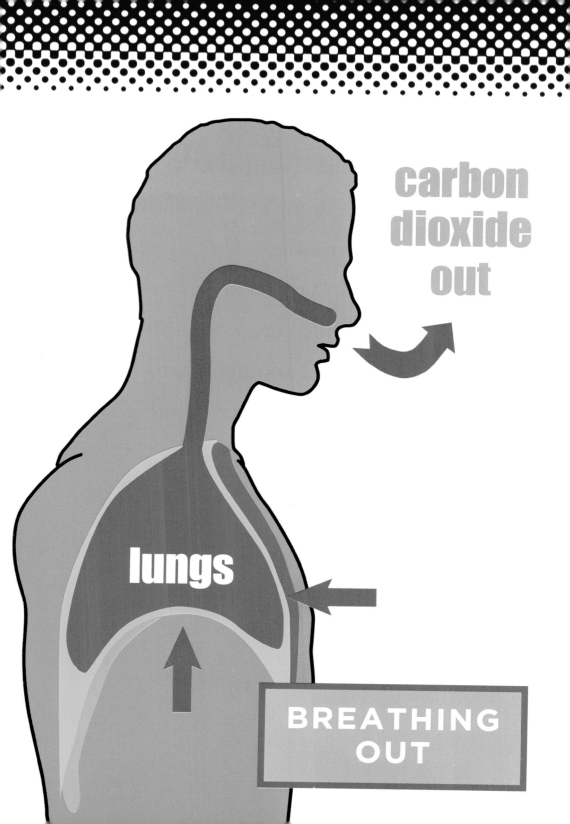

carbon dioxide out

lungs

BREATHING OUT

Getting Waste Out

As blood travels through the body, it makes a stop in the kidneys. These two organs act like **filters**. They catch waste in the blood. Then they send waste and extra water, called urine, to the bladder.

The bladder is another organ. It holds pee until the person can get to a bathroom.

Each kidney is about the size of a fist.

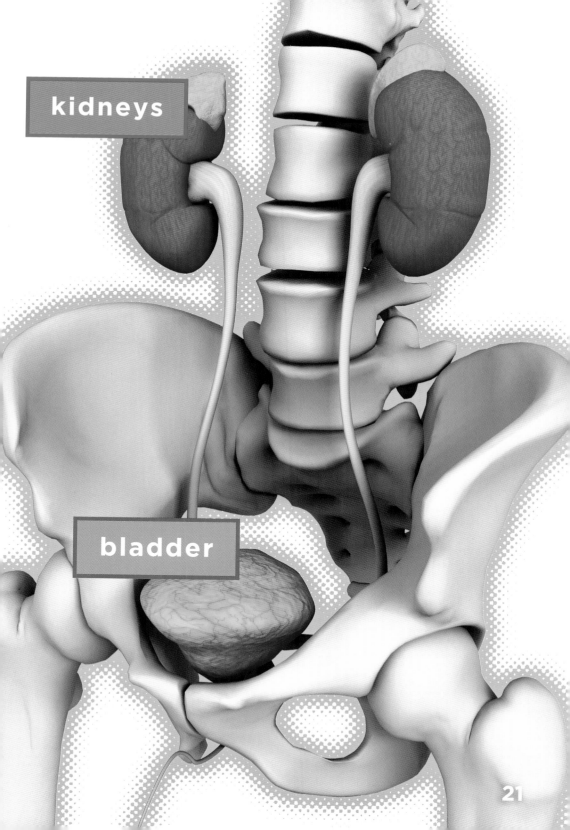

kidneys

bladder

21

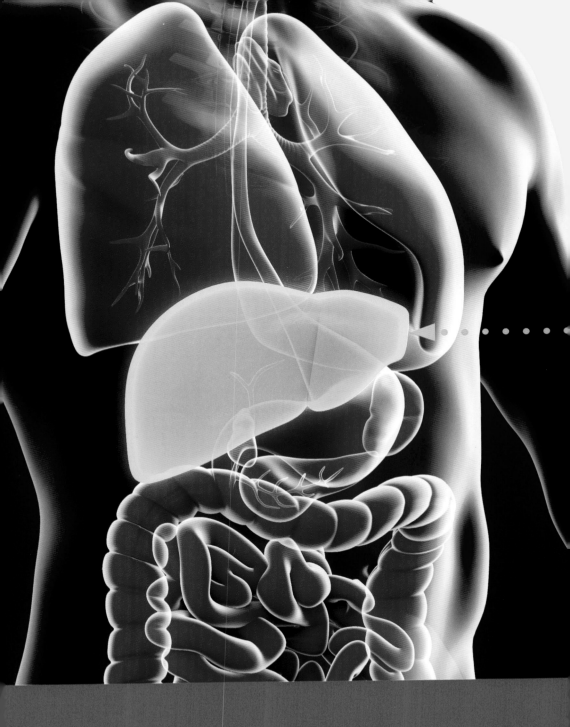

The liver is the only organ that can regrow itself.

CHAPTER 4

Big PROTECTORS

Some organs, like the skin and liver, protect the body. The liver is one busy organ. It breaks down harmful **substances**. It stores nutrients the body needs. And it does more than 500 other things.

The Largest Organ

The skin is the body's largest organ. Its most important job is keeping germs out. It also keeps the body from getting too hot or cold.

SECOND LAYER
makes sweat

THIRD LAYER
keeps the body from getting too warm or cold

Layers of Skin

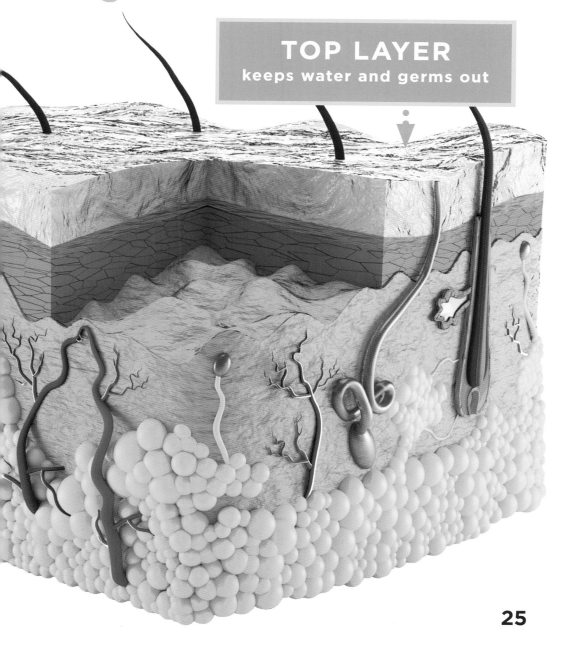

TOP LAYER
keeps water and germs out

CHAPTER 5

Amazing ORGANS

Organs work together to keep the body going. Eating healthy helps keep organs in good shape. Exercise helps keep them strong.

Organs are amazing. This book covered just a few of the body's many organs. Go learn about the rest today!

BY THE NUMBERS

about 20,000
TIMES THE LUNGS BREATHE EACH DAY

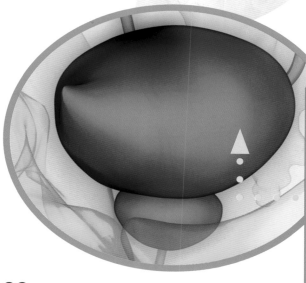

up to
2 cups
(.5 l)
amount of pee an adult's bladder holds

AMOUNT AN ADULT'S STOMACH HOLDS

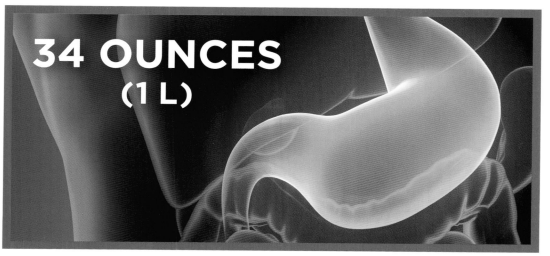

34 OUNCES
(1 L)

up to
20 POUNDS
(9 kilograms)
weight of a
person's skin

about
115,000

TIMES THE HEART BEATS EACH DAY

GLOSSARY

carbon dioxide (KAR-buhn dy-AHK-siyd)—a colorless gas that is formed in the process of breathing

cell (SEL)—one of the tiny units that are the basic building blocks of living things

digest (DY-jest)—to change the food eaten into a form that can be used by the body

electrical (e-LEK-trik-uhl)—made of electricity

filter (FIL-tur)—a substance with pores through which a gas or liquid is passed in order to separate out floating matter

oxygen (AHK-si-jin)—a gas that is necessary for life

pulse (PULS)—a regular throbbing caused by the beating of the heart

substance (SUB-stans)—a physical material from which something is made

BOOKS

Butterfield, Moira and Pat Jacobs. *The Human Body.* Know It All! New York: Cavendish Square, 2016.

Jones, Peter. *The Complete Guide to the Human Body.* New York: Sandy Creek, 2015.

Midthun, Joseph and Samuel Hiti. *Cells to Organ Systems.* Building Blocks of Science. Chicago: World Book, a Scott Fetzer Company, 2014.

WEBSITES

Fun Facts for Kids about Human Body Organs
easyscienceforkids.com/human-body-organs-facts-for-kids-video/

Interesting Facts about Human Organs
www.reference4kids.com/science/interesting_facts_about_human_organs.html

Organs
www.ducksters.com/science/biology/organs.php

INDEX

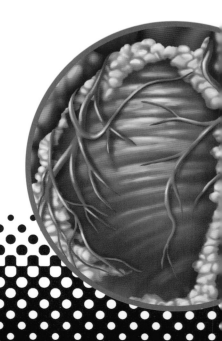